Arts of Truth

Jacob Butkiewicz

To order additional copies of this book, contact:
Xlibris
844-714-8691
www.Xlibris.com
Orders@Xlibris.com

ISBN: Softcover   978-1-6641-5782-8
         EBook   978-1-6641-5783-5

Print information available on the last page

Rev. date: 04/30/2024

1) Knowing wisdom is understanding the foundations of the Universe.

2) No matter how foul the dirt of your life can be, with forgiveness we can be cleansed through the Blood of Christ.

3) We got to encourage one another to come to know Jesus and work for Him.

4) Everybody has their own Blessings they just have to look deep to find them.

5) The ones that are winning are playing in the fields, while the dreamers watch from the stands.

6) The devil can only postpone the righteous from the visualization of their Destiny.

7) We might bear different banners but still serve the same purpose Jesus Christ.

8) Soldiers who give their time, give their Life.

9) If you can't control the beast you won't be Civil.

10) The Piñata is broken spilling candy out into the party; similar to Life, your physical presence is broken through time, to release the traits of your colorful entity.

John 8:12

11) Some can be taught others need miracles.

12) Those who survive the odds are the ones who are Triumphant.

13) Real Friends Understand.

14) Sin is the blindfold that keeps you from seeing the Demonic Firing Squad.

15) You didn't make your foundation, God designed it for you.

16) Happiness is in the hearts of those that preserve life.

17) Haters don't solve problems because they are part of the problem.

18) Wisdom expands beyond structure.

19) I might be judged by the Law of Man, but bound in the end by the Law of God.

20) The Bull will never see the plains if He's always kept in the Barn.

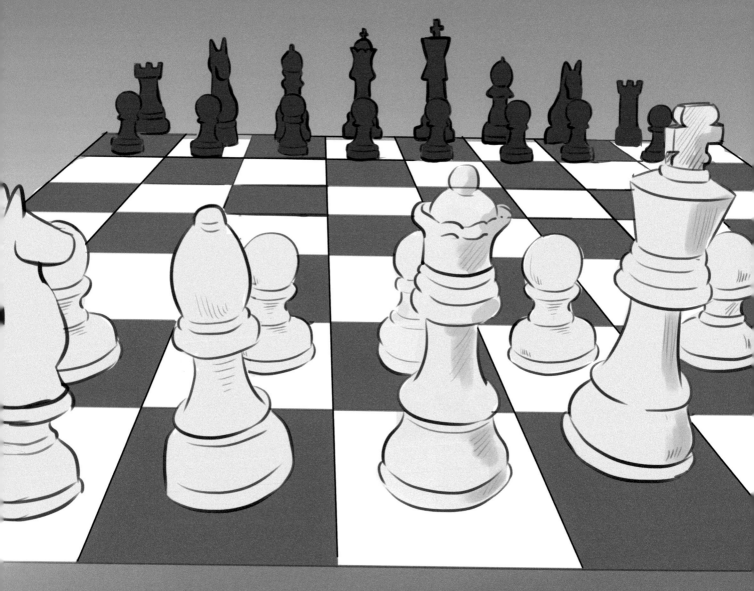

Luke 4:18-19

21) Hate makes you look ignorant.

22) People think its funny how others go through situations; when they lack the experience thinking it could never happen to them.

23) Wisdom surpasses age because Wisdom lives forever.

24) Real Kings go through suffering.

25) When you look in your heart, what do you see?

26) Through Christ, I am.

27) A Samurai sharpens his Katana like a wise man inclines his ear to the truth.

28) Let this sink in your mind and not sit on your desk.

29) It's not that you don't want to work with me, it's the fact you choose not to work with me.

30) A person who hates knows too little.

Mark 16:15-18

31) You have to strain the advice to see what is good.

32) Through the Lords Deliverance people have a future.

33) Anyone who runs from their Love runs from their life.

34) Don't stop running if you see others walking.

35) Hold what is dear & never falter from what is true.

36) Those who boil with hate steam away the essence of their Life.

37) Wisdom speaks in many ways.

38) There's other ways to serve Justice without taking away their Life & Time.

39) Why run from the moment when you're stuck in the time.

40) You don't sell the Lord you give Him Freely.

Luke 6:37

41) Those who run from the Light will fall in the dark.

42) Why stare when you're the one to look at?

43) If you're afraid they're going to leave you; you shouldn't even be there.

44) Don't watch your partner disrespect someone if you know their wrong.

45) Don't let them control you now because they will always be in control.

46) Why do you run from Love when they hold you dear to their heart?

47) The Dust from Ones Life is compressed through the hourglass of time.

48) Money don't last forever so instead of hording it give to others less fortunate as you.

49) Those who suffer, know how to contend against those who stand over them.

50) Why be angry at God when He gave you the chance to be here?

Psalm 18:2

51) I don't want to be based on sin or the talks about it.

52) Why stare into the darkness? When you can see through the Light.

53) I won't have my rest until I won the fight.

54) A good friend stands by you even if you are far apart.

55) The public turns their eye from the truth.

56) If it isn't them, they aren't happy.

57) You got to picture Life without anyone's Arms but God.

58) Real people get corrected.

59) The World plays games.

60) If you don't get it from your family you get it from another.

Deuteronomy 12:28

61) Your hatred isn't going to change nothing about it.

62) Live with Love not with hate.

63) There are a lot of things you didn't know, but it took time to find out.

64) Just because its not on paper doesn't mean it didn't happen.

65) God isn't simple and neither should we.

66) A wedding isn't based on fashion & display it's based on Love.

67) How long you going to sit on it? Till you make it happen?

68) The knowledge of Life is filled by each person who writes it.

69) Knowledge is obtained and wisdom is explored.

70) Its not the discipline that corrects a child, it's the morals and values you daily instill into them.

Proverbs 27:17

71) Its sad to see people attack rather than welcome.

72) Steadfast through the will of God one is guided to fulfill their destiny.

73) 5 Rival Kingdoms clash at War for their Lands, only till each realized they were a Finger of power to equal the palm of one hand.

74) There are so many things we don't see that control our History.

75) We all should look to break bread together.

76) The Squire adheres to Instruction, wielding his blade to stand towards his Knighthood Glory.

77) The White Flowers drop its pedals in the Courtyard while the Bard sings his profound melodies filling the air & soothing the ears.

78) Work towards an agreement, never to be split or separated.

79) Kiss the hands, that you hold dear.

80) Your integrity is placed on the line when you fail to keep your word.

Hebrews 10:35

81) The Fires of hate leave you with nothing.

82) You can't complain if you didn't go the distance.

83) God is my Light that guides me each day.

84) Only through Christ Jesus the way of eternal life, will be paved.

85) When you tear down your team you tear down yourself.

86) How can a child grow if they are not loved?

87) The Master Swordsman engages multiple assailants; enriched by the wisdom & arts of his life teachings. The will of his heart fights to overcome the subjects of the world. Justified by the truth he kneels with Honor facing his destiny.

88) Struggle will lead to enlightenment.

89) The Bells Ring with joy in the pavilion as the children dance around the moonlight glittering with happiness they shine upon their faces.

90) Every mans got to serve his time.

John 14:27

91) The soul speaks louder than the body.

92) My soul kneels towards the Light of God, through His will I grasp the sword of the spirit uplifting my purpose to serve Him.

93) Love brings life and hate brings death.

94) Time doesn't heal all wounds, Christ does.

95) As I walk through the night, I look to the sky. I envision the will of my Father to serve His Hand with pride, destined through the Journey He sees through His Eyes. I clinch my fist to raise honor to the sky, always thankful for the Most High.

96) The Huron warrior with Tomahawk & Knife in hand is outnumbered by enemy soldiers; similar to a Lionheart, by grasping bravery & courage the fiery will of a warrior will take apart every deterrent that stands in his Way.

97) Certain situations in Life need to happen in order for us to break away and be reconnected.

98) Loves got correction.

99) Anyone willing to share their Life with you is Family.

100) We are stronger United divided we get picked apart.

Mark 1:17

Special Thanks

Thank you Lord for always being there for me and getting me through all my times; never giving up on the Love you have for me. Thank you for all the Love and Support I get from my close Family & Friends. Thank you Mom & Dad. Thank you Grandma for always sharing your Love and being there for me. Thank you to the Illustrator: Shannen Marie Paradero, the pictures are Beautiful, thank you so much. Thank you to all my Teammates and future Teammates who want to fight for our Brotherhood/Sisterhood by living to uphold the Lord Jesus by enjoying one another and sharing that time of positivity and good memories. I appreciate you all and I hope one day we can share the same neighborhood, go to different places together, and fight forever for the Lord. RUIN,& HAVC; Thank you for all that you have done to support the Team and be there for me throughout the years. Love & Respect to all the members, to you and your Family's. All of us are important in the eyes of the Lord He Loves us All. All Lives Matter. Just because people make money or have some sort of Worldly status doesn't make them above you. Equal Opportunity for all. Christ lets you see, He Loves us lets us see the Truth for what it is. God is there always standing right behind His one and only Son Jesus Christ. (John 3:16) No matter what you have done Jesus Loves you and has a place for you with Him Forever in Paradise. You have to work hard at everything in order to see the acquired result. Just like that you have to Read the Bible, Pray, Fellowship, and share with others about the importance of having Christ in your Life. Most importantly (Matthew 22:37-40) Christ wants us to Love The Lord God with all your Heart, Soul, Mind, & and Love Our Neighbor as ourselves. Every person is a Lamppost Light your Beacon of Light can spark the Light in others and keep the ground lit so others can follow that light. Be that Light. We All need each other. Were all in this life together, got to make it count. I hope and pray we all can learn from are various life Lessons and Good Times and Memories that we can all be together in Paradise with Jesus Forever. I hope you all are well & safe, God Bless you and yours. Sincerely, Jacob Butkiewicz

If you like this book, you may also
check other books author has written:

The Book of Sayings
The Color of Wisdom
Visions of Truth
The Ant Who Found The Truth

Printed in the United States
by Baker & Taylor Publisher Services